Welcome
to the
Team

NAME

_____

E-MAIL

_____

PHONE

_____

Key Names to Know

NAME	DEPT.	E-MAIL	PHONE

Key Names to Know

NAME	DEPT.	E-MAIL	PHONE

Key Names to Know

NAME	DEPT.	E-MAIL	PHONE

Key Names to Know

NAME	DEPT.	E-MAIL	PHONE

Key Names to Know

NAME	DEPT.	E-MAIL	PHONE

Key Names to Know

NAME	DEPT.	E-MAIL	PHONE

Regularly Scheduled

MEETING	TIME	HOW OFTEN	LOCATION

Meetings to Attend

MEETING	TIME	HOW OFTEN	LOCATION

Regularly Scheduled

MEETING	TIME	HOW OFTEN	LOCATION

Meetings to Attend

MEETING	TIME	HOW OFTEN	LOCATION

Regularly Scheduled

MEETING	TIME	HOW OFTEN	LOCATION

Meetings to Attend

MEETING	TIME	HOW OFTEN	LOCATION

Passwords

WEBSITE	USERNAME	PASSWORD

Passwords

WEBSITE	USERNAME	PASSWORD

Passwords

WEBSITE	USERNAME	PASSWORD

Passwords

WEBSITE	USERNAME	PASSWORD

Passwords

WEBSITE	USERNAME	PASSWORD

Passwords

WEBSITE	USERNAME	PASSWORD

Questions I

Need to Ask

Questions I

Need to Ask

Questions I

Need to Ask

Questions I

Need to Ask

Questions I

Need to Ask

Questions I

Need to Ask

_____

_____

_____

_____

_____

_____

_____

_____

_____

_____

_____

_____

_____

_____

_____

_____

_____

_____

_____

_____

_____

_____

Areas to Improve

Or Make Adjustments

Areas to Improve

Or Make Adjustments

Areas to Improve

Or Make Adjustments

Areas to Improve

_____

_____

_____

_____

_____

_____

_____

_____

_____

_____

_____

_____

_____

_____

_____

_____

_____

_____

_____

_____

_____

Or Make Adjustments

Areas to Improve

Or Make Adjustments

Areas to Improve

_____

_____

_____

_____

_____

_____

_____

_____

_____

_____

_____

_____

_____

_____

_____

_____

_____

_____

_____

_____

Or Make Adjustments

Challenges &

_____

_____

_____

_____

_____

_____

_____

_____

_____

_____

_____

_____

_____

_____

_____

_____

_____

_____

_____

Learning Opportunities

Challenges &

Learning Opportunities

Challenges &

Learning Opportunities

Challenges &

_____

_____

_____

_____

_____

_____

_____

_____

_____

_____

_____

_____

_____

_____

_____

_____

_____

_____

_____

_____

_____

Learning Opportunities

Challenges &

Learning Opportunities

Challenges &

Learning Opportunities

Helpful Tips &

Advice from Co-Workers

Helpful Tips &

Advice from Co-Workers

Helpful Tips &

Advice from Co-Workers

Helpful Tips &

Advice from Co-Workers

Helpful Tips &

Advice from Co-Workers

Helpful Tips &

Advice from Co-Workers

Helpful Tips &

Advice from Co-Workers

Helpful Tips &

_____

_____

_____

_____

_____

_____

_____

_____

_____

_____

_____

_____

_____

_____

_____

_____

_____

Advice from Co-Workers

Helpful Tips &

Advice from Co-Workers

Helpful Tips &

Advice from Co-Workers

Notes

Notes

Notes

Notes

Notes

Notes

Notes

Notes

Notes

Notes

Notes

Notes

_____

_____

_____

_____

_____

_____

_____

_____

_____

_____

_____

_____

_____

_____

_____

_____

_____

_____

_____

_____

_____

Notes

Notes

Notes

Notes

Notes

Notes

Notes

Notes

Notes

Notes

Notes

Notes

Notes